The Ultimate Prepper Checklist

By: Tristan Trouble

Published in USA by:

CDI Publications, LLC
P.O BOX #9
Boynton Beach
FL 33425

© Copyright 2018

ISBN-13: 978-1723352690
ISBN-10: 1723352691

Table of Contents

Introduction

Right now, many of you may be wondering where to begin the process of getting yourself and your family ready for anything and everything that could possibly occur during your lifetime. Topping the list of things you need to be aware of are all the possible hazards that might happen on any given day. There is no short list of expected natural and manmade disasters that can take place with or without forewarning. Most people are familiar with the variety of naturally occurring catastrophes that happen all over the world. We have all either heard of, or in some cases experienced firsthand, hurricanes, tornadoes, tsunamis and other weather related forces of nature. However, many of us have never had the misfortune of being in place when manmade disasters happen, and in many cases, we turn a blind eye to them.

With this educational guide, we hope to provide you with information regarding the various reasons having a good preparation plan in place makes sound, logical sense. A famous proverb states; "Failing to plan is the same as planning to fail," and there is no truer statement when it comes to disaster preparedness.

This is not intended to be a paranoia driven pamphlet. As a matter of fact, it is quite the opposite. When faced with dire circumstances, immediate responsible action needs to be implemented; paranoia, confusion, and uncertainty are the last things you want to deal with. You need to know what to do, how to do it, and when to put your plan into action.

Think of this as an insurance policy. You need to have one in place regardless of previous history and experience because accidents can and do happen when we least expect them. We all have insurance policies in place for the valuable assets we own. Without disaster preparedness plans in place not only are you vulnerable, your family is at increased risk of exposure to tragic events and consequences.

Your primary focus and concern is the safety and security of you and every member of your immediate family. We provide this information, so you can take the necessary steps to ensure everyone is physically, mentally, emotionally, and financially secure should an emergency of any magnitude appear imminent.

In the event a disaster occurs, a standard 72-hour emergency preparedness kit may not contain enough supplies to suitably and effectively keep you and your family safe for the duration of the disaster and beyond.

If you came here looking for a simple, easy to understand and follow, step by step guide to assist you and the family with getting a head start in the disaster and emergency planning process, then congratulations you have come to the right place!

CHAPTER 1: What to Prepare For

Have you thought about where you and your family will be if/when a disaster strikes? Chances are you'll all be in different locations; work, school, running errands, conducting household chores, or on vacation, just to name a few. What will you do? Where will you gather? Different events will require different responses.

Natural Disasters:

Earthquakes—most people have developed a false sense of security with regards to natural disasters of this sort. We fail to realize that this entire planet is made up of tectonic plates. These plates have fault lines for borders. There are enormous primary fault lines as well as smaller secondary ones that are constantly and continuously rubbing and grinding against one another daily. These fault lines weave their way across the face of the entire planet and can affect any of us instantaneously, even in areas without a significant history of earthquakes. This planet wide activity can cause continental shift, volcanic activity, landslides, avalanches, tsunamis, flooding, and in most cases drastic and noticeable changes to the regional topography. They can also have human and environmental impacts including injury and death, as well as damage/destruction of personal property, and interruptions of basic essential services such as water, heat, and electricity, not to mention travel.

Tsunamis—a tsunami occurs when a massive volume of water has been displaced in an ocean. These aquatic anomalies generally take place as a direct result of enormous earthquakes, volcanic eruptions, and detonations that happen below sea level. They can also appear when glaciers give way and slough off into a surrounding body of water. On a lesser scale, tsunamis may rise when a massive landslide, or land mass departure takes place or if/when an interstellar object such as a comet, asteroid, or meteor makes violent impact with the Earth, or a body of water. In all cases involving tsunamis, tidal activity increases to the point normal boundaries of the body of water are breached. Wide spread damage, death, and destruction can occur to the affected ocean basin environment and residents occupying the general vicinity.

Floods—this phenomenon can happen anywhere an abundance of water is present. Flooding occurs when the established boundaries of a body of water are incapable of containing an increase in volume above normal or expected levels. Flooding can occur as a direct result of nature, such as severe torrential storms, and glacial or seasonal runoff due to melting, or even hurricanes. Structural failure of industrial engineering, such as a dam collapse, can also induce flooding in the surrounding basin. On a smaller scale, an unattended bathtub faucet set to run, can induce residential flooding and damage.

Severe Storms & Tornadoes—significant violent weather patterns have been documented on every continent around the world. The same may be said regarding tornadoes except for Antarctica. Without getting too complex and confusing, a tornado appears when drastically opposing warm and cold fronts collide. The colder air descends as the warmer air rises creating a funnel formation that meets the surface of the planet. Depending on the depth and magnitude of this funnel formation, damage and destruction can be minimal or of epic proportions. Results of these severe weather systems can include personal injury or death, property damage or destruction, as well as loss of essential services such as water, electricity, communications, and fuel sources for heat. Complications with the transportation infrastructure may also be present in extreme circumstances.

Hurricanes—this type of intense weather pattern generally affects individuals and environments near coastal regions around the world, normally in the tropical and sub-tropical zones. They begin as smaller storm systems classified as tropical depressions; however, when the conditions are optimal they blossom into increasingly stronger systems, at which time they're upgraded to one of several categories, such as hurricane, typhoon, or cyclone. They can be extremely devastating and unleash havoc on anything in their paths. Personal injury, loss of life, property damage, destruction, and loss of basic essential services are all known to result from these disasters.

Fires—we are all familiar with fire. For centuries it has been considered one of the four elements of nature along with earth, wind, and water. Fire can be produced manually by anyone with the proper instruments and knowledge. It can also be produced through forces of nature such as a lightning strike. Accidental fires are also possible when manmade objects fail or rupture, for instance an exploding electrical transformer. Flammable material, an ignition source, and oxygen are all that are required to start a fire. Fire can spread rapidly under the right conditions and promote hazardous consequences for all animate and inanimate objects in its path, up to and including death and destruction. Fire prevention is just as important as being prepared to handle them.

Winter Storms—this is an area most of us neglect to consider when preparing for disastrous consequences that result from acts of nature. With the increased and often heated debate (no pun intended) surrounding global warming, in conjunction with the apparent reduction in severe winter weather experienced in many regions where excessive annual snowfall amounts were accepted and expected, many of us do not feel the need to prepare for an epic winter storm. Blizzards and ice storms continue to be a force to be reckoned with in several regions of the world.

Winter weather of any magnitude can induce hazardous conditions. Slippery surfaces, such as roads and sidewalks, are the culprits of accidents daily. Extremely heavy snowfall and windy conditions can cause avalanches, structural failures, traffic delays, and accidents involving all modes of transportation within the area, as well as personal injury or loss of life. Blizzards can also bury an area and occupants under a deep and immovable blanket of snow for several days. The loss of basic essential services such as water, communications, electricity, and heat can also complicate matters and induce wide spread panic and fear among the affected.

These are the natural disasters that can occur seasonally around the world which are far beyond our ability to control or manipulate. The safety, security, and general well-being of you and your family will depend on the actions you take today! Attempting to initiate or implement a plan of action, after an event has occurred, almost always results in complete and total failure for everyone involved. The sooner you get with the program and develop an appropriate plan of action, the better off you and your family will be!

Man-made Disasters:

Acts of Terrorism—Contrary to popular belief, terrorism isn't just an international threat, it also needs to be given serious consideration on a national and regional level. Terrorists come from all walks of life. They are usually unidentifiable in the field as they do not tend to advertise their intention until the moment of action. Terrorism is a faceless, nameless entity that makes for a long term adversary.

Most of us couldn't spot a terrorist if they were living across the street. They blend into the surrounding community and conduct themselves accordingly to not draw unwanted attention to their plans and efforts. According to many centralized government agencies and institutions, acts of terrorism happen with little or no forewarning. In other words, we as citizens, are kept in the dark and fed information regarding what happened and why after an atrocity, rather than being informed of the possibility prior to it happening.

An act of terrorism can be carried out by an individual

or by a group. Terrorism has many definitions depending on who uses the term and their immediate understanding of the term. Today, even a schoolyard bully can exhibit tendencies of terrorism by instilling wide spread fear and panic among classmates who are the subject of constant harassment.

Most people relate acts of terrorism to those events that have an impact on a national or international level. The events of 9/11 are what we refer to as international acts of terrorism. The Oklahoma City Bombing, and the actions conducted by the Unabomber, are what we refer to as domestic acts of terrorism. An act of terrorism can also be launched towards a specific person/institution, or an entire population. Terrorist attacks can take place in both the physical world and/or cyber-space.

Terrorism is, in all forms, an act of aggression regardless of the fundamental beliefs of those conducting the crimes. The primary purpose of such an act is to incite fear, panic, and confusion among the affected masses in a given population for whatever reason(s) the inflicting party may have. It is often difficult to prepare for events such as this simply because we do not know how, why, what, or when they are going to occur. Nor do we readily realize the scope of the situation and what it might entail.

Nuclear/Radiological—catastrophes of this nature are something most of us wish we never had to discuss. Those who grew up during the Cold War climate lived in fear of the day hot headed adversaries were going to push the big button and send us all up in a gigantic mushroom cloud of toxic waste. In the modern era, nuclear radiation from fallout is still a very real possibility.

Unfortunately nuclear catastrophes are not solely restricted to detonation of an atomic bomb. Several countries around the world utilize nuclear fusion or fission as a source of energy. These plants are susceptible to rupture/failure, either accidentally through inadequate components and procedures, or because of an act of nature. Accidents involving nuclear power plants do not usually involve the same levels of radiation disbursement as does the detonation of a warhead; however, any leakage of radioactive waste is cause for concern and should be addressed.

Reaction to radiation sickness can include several symptoms, lesions, leaky open sores, ulcers, follicle fallout (hair loss), birth defects, and/or death. The wide spread harmful effects of nuclear disaster, on even a minimal scale, can take decades to recover from. In the event of a global nuclear holocaust, one of two outcomes are possible; the absolute and definitive end of human existence, or the centuries long process of rebuilding and repopulating the planet. It will not be an event you can wait out in the blast bunker for a period of days/weeks before expecting a return to normal activities. If/when it happens, it will be a life altering event of epic proportions, especially for those lucky enough to survive.

Chemical Release—this type of incident is almost always linked to an act of terrorism. An example of this taking place would be the Tokyo subway incident of 1995, in which members of the domestic terrorist organization known as Aum Shinrikyo, released the nerve agent sarin in an unprecedented and coordinated attack involving several separate lines of the mass transportation system simultaneously. Chemical agents of this magnitude have been used as weapons of mass destruction in other parts of the world as well. Reactions to the release of a chemical agent are determined by the lethality of the compound with respect to the quantity being disbursed.

Open sores, leaking blisters, and lesions, upper respiratory issues, loss of vision, loss of motor skills, birth defects, and death are all very real possibilities for anyone subjected to such an environment. Believe it or not, chemical release does not always occur as a direct result of an act of terrorism or war. If you stand over a clogged drain at the kitchen sink and combine two opposing chemical solutions designed to unclog the drain, you could experience many of the same symptoms listed above, up to and including death. Those convenient little warning labels instructing you not to use this item in conjunction with other products from different manufacturers are there for a reason, and it isn't just to protect the manufacturer against claims for liability. They are there for your personal protection more than anything else, read them thoroughly, understand them completely, and adhere to them under all circumstances. Chemical reactions will not only cause the release of toxic and nauseous fumes, they can result in catastrophic explosions, as witnessed in several scientific laboratories during experimentations.

The three topics discussed in this section are referred to as man-made because of the necessity for human interaction/manipulation to bring them to fruition. In other words, they are not things that would occur naturally, with or without the inclusion of humans. We, as humans, are directly responsible for developing these hazardous items and objects, and thereby we are held accountable for any adverse conditions that arise as a direct result of misusing them or promoting them.

While you may or may not have had a hand in the design and development of any or all these potential atrocities, it would be wise of you to be aware of what actions to take should an event happen, as well as being prepared to endure the necessary steps to ensure the survival of self and family! It goes without saying that none of us have the desire to witness any of these events in any way, shape, or form. The fact of the matter is, we do not possess the inherent ability to prevent them should someone else decide to employ them. All we can hope to accomplish is being as prepared as possible to react to a given situation and attempt to survive.

Biological Outbreaks:

Anthrax—a disease that can affect both animals and humans. There are vaccinations and eradication programs that have all but wiped out the ability of this disease to spread as rapidly as it once did. Anthrax is still a highly contagious and devastating disease that has been used as a biochemical agent of war. Exposure to anthrax is almost always lethal, especially if left untreated. It can be contracted through accidental exposure in laboratory experiments, by handling, or encountering infected animals or their hide, or as mentioned above through the release of a biochemical weapon.

Small Pox—for the most part this is not a disease we need to concern ourselves with daily. Due to the increased, extensive, and exhaustive vaccination programs of the 19th and 20th centuries, the World Health Organization in 1979 certified that small pox has indeed been eradicated. There are several unverified reports that small pox bacterium has been hoarded and stored by several government agencies around the world for the specific purpose of developing a weaponized version of the disease that is more resistant to available vaccinations. It is because of these reports we feel it necessary to mention and include it here in this guide.

Plague—a dreadful word that immediately suggests enormous levels of extinction, or massive rates of mortality, and rightfully so. It is a horrendously infectious and often lethal disease. The children's song, "Ring around the Rosie," is often considered to be a folksong associated with the Black Plague in which millions of people all over Europe perished. There are several strains of plague that are still problematic today. There are immunizations available, and early treatment of recognizable cases is almost always successful. So, why is it something we should concern ourselves with? Primarily because it, like several other biologically based diseases, provides the perfect platform for terrorists to stockpile and modify strains for the specific purpose of making them weaponized. Biological warfare makes it possible for one group/faction, to release highly lethal quantities of a disease in a controlled or uncontrolled environment, without being immediately identified as the culprit. Unlike conventional warfare methods, where an enemy can be identified, and targeted, biological devices can be hidden and released over the course of time, allowing the responsible party additional time to escape and remain anonymous.

Flu Virus—who hasn't had some form of flu, or at the very least had an encounter with someone who has had the disease? We are all aware of how contagious it is, and most people are familiar with the commonly associated symptoms of the household flu. There are however several strains that are epidemic and/or pandemic seasonally around the world. Flu vaccinations are normally offered annually here in the United States, especially in the colder regions when fall and winter approach. Why do you need to be aware of what actions to take? Flu viruses can lead to pneumonia, viral or bacterial, both of which can be fatal. In areas where a significant outbreak occurs, quarantine practices and programs are often put into place to assist with control and containment of the illness.

CHAPTER 2: Basic Needs to Create a Family Survival Kit

2.1 Water

Water

Potable—drinking water in other words, it is one of the key life sustaining essentials. Without sufficient drinking water the members of your family will begin to dehydrate, which can cause significant problems, up to and including death. You need to have a few bottles stored in your bug-out bag, or 72-hour kit, you will also need a way to secure additional supplies should your evacuation be of an extended nature. A personal water purification/filtration system for each member of the party is recommended. "Lifestraw," is an excellent and affordable device for serving this purpose.

Non-potable—water that is not suitable for human consumption, but it can be used for other purposes, such as doing laundry, washing dirty dishes, bathing, or watering vegetation. You do not need to bring this type of water along, you will be able to find resources of this nature along the way such as rivers, lakes, and streams. Where you set-up camp should be near an ample supply of non-potable water. It will serve to replenish all your needs with the right purification/filtration equipment.

Purification Tablets—water purification tablets are also an excellent option for inclusion in any emergency evacuation plan. They can be used when the SHTF basic essential services have been compromised or become polluted. These tablets are lighter to carry than bottle or bagged water supplies, thereby providing you with significant resources to replenish your supply wherever you happen to be.

2.2 Food

Food

Non-perishable—this is food that does not require refrigeration for storage, or after it has been opened. Items that fall into this category also have a longer than average shelf life. Your primary focus should be on supplying protein and nutrition. Protein bars are quick and easy to carry and munch on for rapid replenishment of energy. Canned goods are an excellent option for inclusion. Dried goods, such as rice, oatmeal, pasta, and breakfast cereal will provide you with the energy you need to forge on. Box soup mixes, or powdered flavor enhancers, such as beef bouillon cubes, will make bland dried goods more palatable.

Dehydrated food supplies are also worthy of consideration. There are several companies that produce products of this nature. Individuals with previous military experience are familiar with these products in the form of MRE's (Meals Ready to Eat). Many of the items included in these packages can be eaten as they are, while some can be rehydrated with the addition of water. Your evacuation plan should include stockpiling supplies sufficient for sustaining the members of your family for a period of at least three days.

2.3 First Aid Kit

First Aid Kit

Prefabricated Kits—you can purchase a first aid kit that has been professionally assembled by a medical supply company. For families with special needs, supplemental supplies may be necessary to provide appropriate care for the member in question. This is one of the most important items of the evacuation plan regardless of what type of event is taking place. The kit needs to have all the basic supplies that would allow an individual to tend to minor medically related problems that do not require surgical knowledge or expertise. Prefabricated kits are recommended for emergency evacuation plans. They have been put together by people with intimate knowledge of what materials are commonly used for providing medical care for people during disaster scenarios.

Do It Yourself Kits—you can also purchase the supplies for a first aid kit separately and assemble one according to what your needs are. Should you elect to use this method for obtaining a first aid kit, you should make a list of the items you want to include in the inventory. Assembling a first aid kit on your own can result in necessary implements being forgotten or neglected. It is highly recommended you purchase a preassembled kit, and add to it according to your needs, or those of a family member, as this will ensure you have all the items you could need without compromising the integrity of the kit.

CPR—as mentioned previously all members of relative age should be enrolled and attend a certified CPR class. Continued education in this area is also a good idea, as new information and procedures for various injuries are always being added or modified. Refresher courses should be attended every 6 months. Practicing mock-up procedures at home will also ensure everyone in the family is well-equipped and educated in the techniques of the trade.

2.4 Tools & Supplies

Tools & Supplies

Hand Tools—a selection of manual hand tools will be essential for your survival. Tools that have interchangeable functioning parts, such as screwdrivers with various bits carried in the handle, an adjustable wrench, etc. occupy less space in emergency kits and allow for greater freedom of use. They will also come in handy during emergency events in which energy resources have been compromised.

Power Tools—a selection of corded electrical tools

should be stocked and stored at the bug-out facility, but only if there is a power supply source on site. They are too heavy and cumbersome to carry in emergency preparedness kits; however, they may come in very useful under the right circumstances and situations.

Battery Operated Tools—tools of this nature are powered by large batteries connected directly to the device. There are several companies that manufacture items of this nature. Kits containing drills, drivers, and saws can be found at any of the major name brand home improvement centers. They can also be found at most local hardware stores or purchased online.

Additional Supplies—Nylon rope and climbing equipment is gear you may want to consider. Traveling over rough and rugged terrain is a very likely possibility; you will need the right gear for navigating through, around, or over these areas. Rope will also come in handy should you need to drag or tow something behind you or hang clothing for drying.

Snow shoes might also be something you need should

your evacuation involve traveling by foot through winter weather. Most of the gear and supplies you will need have been listed in other sections of this guide. The region in which you and your family live, may determine additional gear you want to consider. For instance, residents of places like Seattle, Washington may find rain ponchos and wet weather gear a necessity, as this area tends to see a significant amount of rain annually.

Cell phones, tablet computers, or other mass media storage devices may serve the purpose of storing data. Much of the contact information listed above regarding names, addresses, phone numbers, and email accounts are already stored on these personal devices. If they cannot be recharged due to power failure, then they should be used moderately and only for securing necessary information. Turn them off when not in use and conserve battery life. Disposable heating implements, such as those you can insert in your gloves and boots for additional warmth, might be something you want too.

2.5 Clothing & Bedding

Clothing & Bedding

Clothing—a change of clothes is necessary. Nothing tends to complicate matters, or make them more uncomfortable, than trying to make passage from one point to another with damp or saturated clothes. Consider quick drying fabrics for this, as they will allow you to continue your travel plans with minimal interference or interruption. Your clothing should be lightweight, yet suitable for existing environmental conditions. You will need at least one complete set of clothes to change into. You will also want a change of clothes available for the specific purpose of accommodating rapid weather changes. You might leave the house dressed for warmth yet find yourself overly dressed for the conditions that arise along the route. Your clothes should be comfortable for traveling under any conditions.

Bedding—this needs to be adequate and sufficient, if not entirely comfortable. It should also be lightweight, as you may have to shoulder the burden of carrying it on your back, in the event you are forced to continue by foot. While a good night's rest will replenish your body, and make you better equipped to handle the following day's events, emergency situations tend to heighten the senses of those affected. Chances are, even a king size bed with pillow top mattress, is not going to keep you from tossing, turning, and coming awake at the smallest snap of a twig or noise in the bush. The primary area of concern is making sure the bed is off the ground. Do not sleep directly on the ground!

2.6 Special Items

Special Items

For Infants—babies and toddlers will require special equipment in an emergency. A three day's supply of all the essentials they normally use will be necessary. Powdered formula, or dry cereal mixtures, that they eat daily will need to be included. Families that are breast feeding should include supplemental food supplies, a breast pump, and disposable bottle feeding systems, to provide for their children as it may not always be possible to stop along the route when the child needs to be fed. Any medications they are currently taking, prescription or OTC, should be brought along.

Several changes of clothing will also be necessary. Babies and small children are uncoordinated and messy with their eating habits. Clothing, soiled by food stains, will be the equivalent of bait for predatory animals in the area. These garments need to be removed and rinsed free from food particles, then replaced with fresh clean accommodations. Diapers are going to be an area of concern as well. While disposable diapers can be disposed of along the route, carrying a three day supply of them in conjunction with cleaning equipment such as wipes, will add an enormous amount of weight to the emergency preparedness kit. Consider using cloth diapers for the evacuation procedure. They can be washed, dried, and reused, reducing the amount of weight you are carrying while still providing for the needs of the child. Ointments and powders, for curing or controlling the outbreak of diaper rash, will also be required. Small containers of these topical treatments are all you will need to make the trip. A papoose, or baby carrying backpack, is also something that should be given serious thought. Should you have to travel by foot, cradling a baby or child in your arms, is not going to be in your best interest. Babies and small children are the responsibility of everyone in the family, and a rotating schedule for feeding and transporting them should be implemented, to reduce the stress on a single person.

For Children—pre-teen members of the family also have special needs or desires in an emergency. They often want to help in any way possible. The fact of the matter is they are normally ill-equipped, with respect to strength and knowledge, to be of significant use in many scenarios. You will need to bring along a few children's books for reading and entertainment to keep them occupied in the event your attention needs to be focused elsewhere without interruption. A coloring book and crayons might also be placed in the bag for the same purpose of keeping them distracted during crucial times. Consider allowing them to bring along a favorite toy, stuffed animal, or blanket. These items are usually considered a security device for the child, providing comfort in uncertain times. If serviceable, let them bring along digital media storage devices, such as an mp3 player, tablet computer, or similar device, for providing additional entertainment. All medications they are taking, prescription or OTC, should also be included as well as any special needs equipment they require.

For Adults—Any and all medications, prescription or OTC, should be included. Small objects of a sentimental nature might also be included if they do not compromise the plan. Adults are going to be the primary beasts of burden in most emergency situations. They will be accountable and responsible for ensuring the security and safety of the family unit. Depending on the nature of the event, and the availability of essential services, technological devices such as a laptop, tablet, or smart phone, may be imperative to being able to conduct business as usual under extraordinary circumstances. Most items listed in this guide will be used or prepared by the adults in the clan. Additional non-essential items and objects add unnecessary weight to the emergency kits, thereby slowing down the progress of the entire family; they should therefore be avoided unless necessary.

Important Family Documents—some of the items that make this list can be found in previous sections of this guide. Originals and photo copies of personal identification for each member of the family should be brought along.

Personal Documents

- Birth Certificates
- Adoption Papers
- Citizenship/Naturalization Papers
- Military Discharge Papers
- Last Will
- Trust Documents
- Burial Instructions (instructions or arrangements that have been previously made)
- Safe Deposit Boxes and/or Safes (keys/combinations)
- Powers of Attorney
- School Records
- Earned Educational Degrees

Financial Accounts Information

- Bank/Credit Union Accounts (Checking, Savings)
- Retirement Accounts
- Brokerage Accounts
- Pension System Statements
- Deferred Compensation Papers
- Credit Card Accounts
- U.S. Savings Bonds
- Money Market Accounts
- Certificates of Deposit (CDs)
- Stock Certificates/Bonds

Financial Papers

- Real Estate Deeds

- ❖ Mortgage Documents
- ❖ Property Tax Records
- ❖ Inventory of Assets
- ❖ Vehicle Titles
- ❖ Income Tax Returns for Several Years
- ❖ Rental/Lease Agreements
- ❖ Partnership Agreements
- ❖ Outstanding Loans
- ❖ Pending Legal Actions/Lawsuits

Medical & Health Insurance

- ❖ Health Care Provider and Personal ID Number
- ❖ Mortgage Insurance Policy
- ❖ Long Term Care Policy Information
- ❖ Organ Donor Information
- ❖ Living Will/Health Care Proxy
- ❖ Life Insurance Policy Documents
- ❖ VA Insurance Policy
- ❖ Property and Casualty Policies
- ❖ Medical Records
- ❖ Immunizations
- ❖ Prescriptions
- ❖ List of OTC Medications (currently being taken)

Note: You should have the originals of all documents stored in a portable water tight safe carried in plastic zip-lock bags for additional protection. Color photo copies of these should also be carried in plastic zip-lock bags in the event the originals are unavailable or become damaged, destroyed, lost, or stolen. You should also make a list of names, numbers, and pertinent contact information, for your personal accountant, attorney, and/or financial advisor. These instruments of identification are vital to us in several ways; without them, being able to function at any level near normalcy will be difficult, if not entirely impossible. Depending on the circumstances some of these documents will be necessary to gain access or passage through checkpoints, border crossings, etc.

CHAPTER 3: Beyond the Basic Needs

3.1 Plan to Expand

Plan to Expand

- **Two Weeks**
  - Initial supplies. Immediate resources. After building a 72 hour plan, expand and stockpile enough gear and supplies for 2 weeks. Use the same checklists provided in this guide.
- **One Month**
  - Extended stays. Once you've hit the 2 week mark, go ahead and grow a little more, gather the goods and gear to get you through an entire month. This may also include having enough supplies to care for a handful of unexpected others.
- **Three Months**
  - Extended stays. Going beyond the one month mark, extend your plan to include enough food, water, and essentials to cover your family for an entire 3 month period.
- **Six Months**
  - Extended stays above and beyond expectations. Next comes the 6 month mark!

- **One Year**
    - Extended stays under dire circumstances or world changing events. After reaching the 6 month mark, the one year mark will provide for you and your family in the event society completely collapses.
- **Beyond**
    - Resources for surviving nuclear holocaust, or interstellar earth impacting events. Ensures essentials are available until such a time as they can be replenished through hunting, gardening, and foraging techniques.

Note: Remember, if you're stockpiling perishable food and potable water, then you will need to rotate that into your current supply and restock as necessary.

3.2 Develop a Survivalist Mindset

Develop a Survivalist Mindset

- **Expect the Worst**
    - Never assume things will be the same after a disaster strikes. Be prepared for the possibility of damage, destruction, or total loss of property, as well as life, intimate as well as associative.
- **Plan for the Worst**
    - See above. Have a plan in place or available in the event you should need to file claims for compensation and rebuild from the

ground up. Be prepared to suffer the eternal loss of valuable items that cannot be replaced. Know what to do and when to do it. Have available policies and contact information at your disposal. Checklists will come in handy to determine what has been lost, what remains, what needs to be replaced or repaired, as well as what needs to be reported to the appropriate authority, such as gas leaks, downed power lines, failed electrical equipment, ruptured water delivery and drainage systems. Be prepared to set-up temporary shelter near the residence until it is approved for occupancy. Seek assistance from available resources in the community. Volunteer to assist if/when you can with any search and rescue, or rebuilding efforts. Take the most devastating disaster you are preparing for and multiply expectations by 10, then plan accordingly.

✦ Learn Your Skills

- Read relevant material
- Make checklists for everything of interest
- Inventory items to determine what you have
- Secure items missing from the list
- Practice mock-up drills for all disasters relative to your region
- Refresh education periodically
    - Revisit web sites to read additions and modifications
    - Attend training seminars or classes
- Develop those skills

- Practice them until they are second nature
- Physically perform every aspect of training
- Repetition breeds confidence

Learn Your Equipment

- Purchase it
- Read the instruction manual front to back
- Perform various tasks with the equipment
- Make sure it is in good working order
- Learn how to repair minor problems
- Use creativity
  - Envision other ways you could use the device to substitute for items not in the inventory
- Research manufacturer web sites to discover more in depth knowledge about how the items are made, what materials are being used, how they might come in handy for constructing other useful tools and machinery, etc.

3.3 Additional Education / Learn a Trade

Additional Education/Learn a Trade

The checklist below features preparedness skills and or trades that would be useful under the dire circumstances of a post disaster scenario. We recommend learning as many of these as possible and teaching them to your kids.

- **Canning**
  - Food Preservation & Storage
  - Longer Shelf Life
- **First Aid**
  - Essential in all disaster scenarios; cannot be neglected
- **Emergency Response Training**
  - Military Field Medicine (ex. Israeli Tourniquet)
  - Paramedic Training
  - CPR
  - Fire Rescue & Recovery
  - Rapid Water Rescue & Recovery
- **Material Fabrication**
  - Wood Working
  - Metal Working
  - Leather Tanning
  - Sewing
- **Engineering**
  - Mechanical Repair
  - Electrical Repair
  - Engine Repair
  - Building & Construction
  - Irrigation
    - Water Retrieval
    - Water Purification
    - Water Delivery
  - Harnessing Alternative Energy Resources
    - Solar
    - Wind
    - Water

+ **Gardening**
  - Crop Raising
  - Crop Harvesting
  - Herbal Medicine
  - Identifying Useful & Harmful Plant Species
+ **Self-Defense**
  - Martial Arts
  - Close Quarters Combat
  - Small Weapons Classes
  - High Caliber Weapons Instruction
  - Defensive Fortifications
  - Evasive Maneuvers (from man and wildlife)
  - Cover & Concealment
+ **Hunting & Harvesting Animals**
  - Hunting Small Game
  - Hunting Large Game
  - Preparing & Processing Animal Flesh
  - Raising Livestock
  - Slaughtering & Processing Livestock
  - Curing & Storage Methods
+ **Fishing**
  - Conventional Fishing
  - Fish Traps
  - Fish Nets
  - Unconventional Fishing
+ **Foraging Wild Edibles**
  - Identifying Edibles
  - Identifying Toxic Plants
  - How to perform an Edibility Test

3.4 Long Term Water Storage

Long Term Water Storage

When it comes to water you're going to need a ton of it; it's the first thing to disappear from grocery store shelves when local water resources become contaminated. Water is extremely heavy. We do not recommend storing massive amounts of water at home unless you plan on bugging in no matter what the situation is; otherwise you may have to bug-out, and you won't be carrying anywhere near 55 gallons of water with you.

- **Larger Containers**
  - Secure 15, 30, & 55 gallon food grade plastic drums
    - Store potable water in these
  - Secure 55 gallon stainless steel drums for heating large quantities
    - Bathing
    - Laundry
    - Doing Dishes

If you do have to bug-out, you may need to build a few of these systems to use water without having to shoulder it bucket by bucket from one place to another.

⊥ Retrieval & Delivery Systems
- Irrigation Ditches
- Syphoning Pumps
- Building a Water Wheel
- Building Bathing Equipment

If you do have to bug-out, you might also find yourself needing to use nothing but natural resources. In that case you will need to locate it, as well as be able to filter and purify it.

⊥ Finding & Filtering Resources
- Natural Resources in close proximity
  - Clear running waterways, rivers, streams (preferred)
  - Lakes, Ponds, Stagnant Water (last resort)
  - Rain Collecting Equipment
  - Seasonal Runoff Collecting Equipment
- Personal Filtration/Purification Devices for everyone in the family
- Water Purification Tablets
- Shock Chlorination Techniques
- Charcoal Filtration Systems

3.5 Long Term Food Storage

Long Term Food Storage

Food is the second thing to disappear off grocery store shelves. You can avoid the mad dash and fight for groceries by stockpiling them now, or by growing your own garden and preserving your surplus, which we highly recommend if you have the land and means available.

- **Shop Smart**
  - Buy in Bulk
    - Dry Goods
    - Canned Goods
    - Non-perishable Food Items
  - Warehouse Distributors
  - Grain Elevators (Animal Feed)
  - Purchase Seed Stock
  - Hunt & Trap
  - Fish
    - Harvest, Clean & Prepare

If you need storage containers for your bulk food purchases, here are some of the ideas we recommend.

- **Larger Containers**
  - Plastic or Metal
  - Lined with plastic bags

- Securable Covers
- Small Scale Grain Silos (Animal Feed)
- Meat Lockers

3.6 Permanent Vehicle Survival Kit

Permanent Vehicle Survival Kit

Don't think you need a vehicle emergency kit? Here are just a few of the reasons one could come in handy.

- **Stranded in an Emergency**
  - Traffic congestion (stuck in traffic for hours while an accident gets cleaned up)
  - Run out of fuel
  - Mechanical vehicle failure (something breaks down)
  - Lost along the route
  - Complications along a route
  - Trapped in a flood
  - Trapped in a blizzard
- **Your Vehicle Becomes Your Only Available Shelter**
  - Permanent/Temporary shelter not ready
  - Shelter has been compromised
  - Reaching shelter is impossible
  - Secondary shelter has collapsed
  - Lost/Stranded in unfamiliar territory
- **Items to Keep in Kit**
  - Vehicle Bug-out Bag
  - Additional Fuel Supplies

- Blankets & Bedding
- Warm & Cool Weather Clothing
- 3 Day Supply of Non-perishable Food
- Water Purification Equipment
- Heating Implements
    - Disposable Lighter
    - Matches
- Extra Pair of Shoes
- Automotive Repair Tools & Manuals
- Vehicle Jacking Equipment
- Flashlights/Lanterns
- Tow Grade Rope
- Duct Tape
- First Aid Kit
- 3 Day Supply of Prescription Medication
- Identification Documents
- Maps
- Compass
- GPS (if serviceable)
- Flares
- Small Caliber Handgun (personal protection; hunting small game; signaling device)
- Whistle
- Communications Equipment (cell phone may not be serviceable, hand crank radios for listening to the airwaves, as well as hand crank base camp radios or walkie talkies should be considered)
- Hand Tools
    - Axe/Hatchet
    - Shovel

- Rope & Climbing Gear
- Utility Knife
- Pocket knife
- Hunting Knife
- Bow & Arrows (optional for hunting larger game)
- Jumper Cables
- Spare Spark Plugs
- Spare Tire
- Spare Fuses
- Spare Battery (fully charged)

3.7 Survival Gear & Equipment

Survival Gear & Equipment

This is a generalized list of survival gear and equipment. There are several manufacturers to choose from; we recommend getting gear that big enough to provide for you and your family. For instance, small collapsible hobo stoves can be considered wood burning stoves, but they aren't going to be big enough cook a meal for 4-5 people.

- **Stove & Fuel**
  - Wood Stoves
    - For Cooking (cast iron; log burning)
    - For Warmth (pellet or grain burning)
      - Small log burning (like fireplace inserts)

- Gas Stoves
    - Propane (natural gas and/or electricity may be unavailable)

Camping Equipment

- Better or Bigger Tents
- Cooking Utensils
    - Cast Iron
    - Stainless Steel
    - Tripods (for hanging kettles or grills)
    - Dutch Oven
    - Roasting Spit

Sleeping Supplies

- Better Sleeping Bags (zero weather gear)
- Enclosed Hammocks
- Sleeping Cots
- Air Mattresses
- Permanent Beds (for the shelter)
- Softer Pillows (for shelter use)

Inclement Weather Gear

- Rain Ponchos
- Rubber Boots
- Arctic Climate Clothing
    - Hats
    - Boots
    - Pants
    - Jackets
    - Gloves
    - Facial Masks
    - Snow Shoes
    - Safety Goggles
- Pocket Warmers

- Quick Dry Clothing (wet weather or humid conditions)

↓ Lighting Equipment
- Gas/Oil Lamps
- Hand Crank Flashlight
- Fuel Torches (handmade from available resources)
- Fire Starting Utensils
- Glow Sticks
- Solar Powered Substitutes

↓ Communications Equipment
- Ham Radios
- Hand Crank Base Camp Radios
- Hand Crank Portable Walkie Talkies

↓ Hunting & Fishing Equipment
- Large Caliber Rifles
- Small Caliber Rifles
- Knives
  - Hunting
  - Fishing
- Traps
  - Fishing Seines
- Rods & Reels
- Line & Baits
- Fishing Hooks

↓ Cutting Implements
- Axes
- Saws
- Hatchets
- Chainsaw

⊥ Other Items of Interest

- Rope
    - Nylon
    - 550 Parachute Cord
- Climbing Equipment
    - Grappling Hooks
    - Safety Helmets
    - Harnesses
    - Carabineers
    - Gloves
    - Boots
    - Safety Goggles
- Personal Watercraft
    - Canoes
    - Kayaks
    - Rubber Rafts
    - Small John Boat with Oars
- Towing Equipment
    - Wagons
    - Sleds

3.8 Emergency Cash Cache

Emergency Cash Cache

We always recommend financial diversification, especially as a back-up to fiat paper currencies. Precious metals like gold and silver can be found in certain coins, like Kruggerands. These make a good investment because they are easy to store and use; even if the additional metal alloy in the coin is considered worthless, the silver or gold can be extracted and still hold value. Precious gems may or may not hold value in a post-collapse scenario.

- **Precious Metals**
  - Gold
  - Silver
  - Platinum
- **Precious Gems**
  - Diamonds
  - Emeralds
  - Rubies
- **Paper Currency**
  - Small Denominations in the amount of $1,000.00
    - Ones & Fives (change may not be available)

+ **Coin Currency**
  - Rolled Quarters (highest value of commonly carried coins)

__Note:__ Currency of any kind may become completely devalued in a post-apocalyptic environment. Many believe various bartering systems will replace the current method of exchanging goods and services for paper or precious metals. It will however come in handy for most disaster scenarios and should therefore be included in all preparedness plans where feasible.

3.9 Associate with Others

Associate with Others

Prepping is not a solo sport; even if you're the only one in your family who is actively participating, you're doing it for your family. They might think you're crazy now, but if disaster ever strikes they're going to be thankful you've done what you can to keep them safe. Here are some ideas on becoming a better prepper!

+ **Build a Community of Like Minded Individuals**
  - Visit local disaster preparedness centers
  - Attend meetings and functions
  - Socialize with members you meet at these sessions
  - Schedule additional separate meetings and events

- Research regional news media and advertisements
  - Homesteaders
  - Off the Grid Enthusiasts
  - Emergency Preparedness Specialists
- Join Respective Social Networking Groups
- Secure and provide contact info for all new acquaintances

Involve Them in Planning

- Assign tasks and responsibilities
- Provide or recommend training
- Discuss, debate, and agree on processes and procedures

Incorporate & Implement

- Pick their brains
- Encourage creativity
- Include any significant ideas they bring to the table
- Adjust the plan
- Ensure everyone is made aware of changes
- Practice mock-up exercises
  - Localized (family members and close associates)
  - Regional (consisting of all citizens concerned)

Government Sponsored Community Programs

- Visit your local county disaster preparedness office
- Visit Red Cross facility/web site
- Visit FEMA web site

- Visit Coast Guard web site (some natural disasters strike while at sea or in coastal regions)
- Volunteer to participate
    - Get familiar with how governing bodies conduct business during a massive event
- Visit the local EMS/Fire & Rescue
    - Research and discover their practices and first response procedures

Note: *Government sponsored disaster prep and rescue programs are extremely educational and informational, their practices and procedures have derived from handling similar situations around the country or the planet. They constantly update their information and modify techniques to better equip themselves and the average citizen in the event a catastrophe occurs. A great deal of what you learn from these programs can be directly implemented into your own disaster survival solutions.*

3.10 Encourage Family & Friends

Encourage Family & Friends

This is pretty much self-explanatory; try to get them involved, but don't be pushy to the point it causes problems. If disaster ever strikes they'll get on board quicker than you think.

- **Explain Your Actions**
  - Discuss with them why you feel it is necessary to prepare for an event
  - Inform them how you came to this conclusion
  - Share all relevant information with them
  - Host group sessions for disbursing information
- **Advantages & Disadvantages**
  - Show them how preparing benefits them even if they never have to use it
  - Advertise it as an insurance policy (that is in effect what it is)
  - Share statistical data to support your claims
  - Explain to them the disadvantages
    - Less chance of survival
    - Greater chance of injury or death
    - Affects it will have on others (extended family members & friends)
- **Offer to Include Them**
  - Extended Family Members
    - Financially unable to make accommodations
    - Elderly incapable of arranging adequately for themselves
    - Younger children of your siblings
  - Encourage them to participate

CHAPTER 4: Protecting Family & Possessions

4.1 Low Profile Tactics

Low Profile Tactics

Cover / Concealment—in some environments or scenarios it will be necessary to remain hidden or incognito. If you stick out like a sore thumb, then you will be easy to target, identify, and remember by all those you encounter. Camouflage clothing in wilderness environments will allow you to blend into the natural surroundings. Camouflaging the shelter in these outdoor situations might also be a necessary inclusion in your survival plans to prevent unwanted attention. **This does not apply to all disaster preparedness plans or emergency scenarios.**

Suburban Blending—like the cover and concealment techniques mentioned above for areas of an urban or suburban nature. You need to blend in with the members of the community. Discard the camouflage and BDU/ACU's (Battle Dress/Army Combat Uniform) approach in these environments. Alter any military style appearance including haircut and facial grooming techniques so that you look like an average citizen. Civilians often associate members of the military with having extensive training in survival tactics; they may try to tag-along or tail your movements to ambush and rob you of supplies just for looking like you've had military training.

Why *is this necessary*—not everyone surviving a disaster is going to be of the same mindset. Several survivors will be ill prepared to provide for themselves. They will seek out supplies and resources. Anything they find attractive or lucrative becomes a possible target. Some of these survivors will develop a pack animal mentality. They will hunt and gather together, overpowering their subjects with brute force if necessary. Being able to avoid these situations will be to your benefit. Even if you survive an encounter of this nature, chances are it will be at the surrender of your supplies and equipment, at which point your chances of survival have just diminished and left you among the destitute.

4.2 Avoid Initial Bartering

Avoid Initial Bartering

Saving Your Supplies—nobody can predict with any accuracy how devastating a disaster is going to be, nor can they pinpoint the length of time it will last. You'll want to save what supplies you have to ride out the storm. You put together your survival cache of supplies to ensure you could make the journey from one location to another. You have no idea what lies ahead. Unforeseen circumstances could complicate your original plans to such a degree even your back-up plan(s) are ineffective. It might take longer than expected to arrive at the location of your second shelter and additional supplies. If you have packed your equipment accordingly, and followed your bug-out plan, you shouldn't need to barter for additional supplies right away.

Avoid Unwanted Attention—keeping your supplies to yourself will also help you maintain a low profile. You do not want to be known for flaunting your valuables around in an open trade market. This will draw unwanted attention to you and your belongings. People will want the things you have, they just won't want to pay or trade for them. You will ultimately paint a target on your back, and your bag, and may have to defend yourself to ensure survival.

__Note:__ You should never leave your supplies unattended. If your journey includes several days travel you will have to locate areas of cover and concealment to store your bag while you are sleeping, scouting, hunting, or gathering additional supplies. Depending on the size of the family, and age of members, a rotating watch during sleeping schedules may be necessary.

4.3 Do I Need a Firearm?

Do I Need a Firearm?

Purposes & Uses—there are several areas where a firearm might come in handy, personal protection of you, your family, and your supplies being the most obvious. People react to disastrous events abnormally. In other words, normal personal conduct during these situations alters drastically. Some become meek, mild, and scared; others become courageous, daring, or violent. You have no idea what mentality you will encounter. Other survivors are going to be carrying personal arsenals as well. You do not want to encounter a potential adversary unequipped to fend for those in your care. Nobody shows up to a gun fight carrying a pocket knife with hopes of being victorious; don't be caught empty handed or without effective and defensive weaponry.

Hunting & Harvesting—a firearm will make hunting easier to accomplish than trapping and hand killing an animal. It will also come in handy should you need to forage for nuts, berries, or edible foliage. Predatory wildlife may be present in the area and searching for a food source themselves. If you are unprotected, you might make an appealing appetizer for carnivorous wildlife.

Trade & Bartering—firearms can also fetch a hefty price on an exchange market established in a post collapse community. Depending on how long it takes to rebuild having items of value will be essential to making it though the long term effects of the rebuilding phase.

Firearms Options—handguns come in a wide range of calibers. For initial purposes a small caliber handgun such as a .22 or .38 is recommended. They are lightweight compared to higher calibers and ammunition is cheaper and easier to carry in huge quantities. Small caliber handguns are also easier to keep concealed.

A shotgun is another option. Less effective over long distances yet extremely lethal at close range. They are harder to conceal and more cumbersome to carry. Ammunition is much larger than other firearm options and therefore not as efficient to carry in mass quantities.

The rifle is also an option that involves additional

weight and restrictions. They are almost impossible to conceal, can be spotted from long distances, and are not as maneuverable in close quarters combat situations. They do allow for shooting over longer distances but that is only advantageous in a few scenarios.

__Note:__ Large caliber weapons, rifles, shotguns, and weapons are something that should be included in the bug-out shelter. Your initial travel arrangements need to focus on stealth and swiftness. The less you must carry and account for, the quicker you will arrive at your destination.

Firearms Education—before anyone loads a firearm and pulls a trigger for the first time it is highly recommended they attend a firearm's safety class and receive general education regarding how to properly, effectively, and safely operate a firearm. Handling, care, and maintenance of a firearm is just as important as pointing it down range and engaging a trigger with pinpoint accuracy. In addition to firearm's safety training, it will also be necessary for all those carrying a weapon to develop the right mentality with respects to using it for personal protection. You do not have to have a warrior or murderous instinct, but you must be prepared to take a life if necessary. When the chips fall on the table, will you be able to ensure you are the last one standing?

CHAPTER 5: Building a Disaster Preparedness Family Plan

The following checklists should help you research and discover information that pertains to you and your situation. They may also be used to ensure all recommendations for emergency preparedness have been followed.

5.1 Research and Do Your Planning Homework

Research and Do Your Planning Homework

Learn About Likely Disasters in Your Area

- Visit the local county disaster preparedness center/office
- Check historical weather records for the region
- Research & discover locations of nuclear power plants
- Research & discover locations where hazmat substances are manufactured or stored
- Check historical records for natural disasters familiar to the region

Familiarize the Family of Alerts & Alarms

- Research & discover where sirens and alarms are located
- Find out what the warning signals and sirens are for your region
- Simulate these sounds, alarms, and sirens
- Develop similar methods of communicating locally (whistles, lights, coded messages)

Learn Proper Response Procedures

- Request and secure literature pertaining to regional responses
- Develop a "Buddy System" to ensure everyone is accounted for
- Practice response techniques as a family unit
- Educate younger family members frequently
- Focus on proper procedures and modify any areas of interest
- Adapt response procedures to compensate for obstacles

Federal, State, & Local Assistance Programs

- Research federal disaster preparedness web sites such as FEMA
- Visit the Red Cross web site to locate the regional office
- Visit the county disaster prep center
- Research state associated web sites related to Emergency Management

- Visit the Department of Homeland Security web site
- Visit the local EMS and Fire Station

Learn Response Procedures for Places of Interest

- Work
- School
- Daycare
- Other areas the family frequents regularly

Develop a Complete List of Personal Contact Info

- Names, addresses, email, landline, and cellular numbers for the following
  - Doctors
  - School
  - Daycare
  - Place of work
  - Family, friends, and relatives

5.2 Make Checklists & Update Them Often

Make Checklists & Update Them Often

Update Emergency Contact Info

- Fire
- Police
- EMS
- Immediate family & friends

Look for Home Hazards

- Check and secure windows
- Check and secure doors
- Eliminate obstacles from commonly used hallways and passages
- Make sure all stairs or steps are in good working order
- Establish evacuation exits from various rooms

Locate Safe Zones in Home or on Property

- Basements
- Bathtubs
- Panic Rooms
- Cellars
- Subterranean Storm Shelters
- Reinforced Crawl Spaces

Inventory & Replenish Disaster Supplies

- Identify supplies you already have
- Make a list of supplies you still need
- Find places for purchase
- Obtain items on list
- Build Disaster Preparedness Kit
- Replace expired supply stock

Learn Basic First Aid & CPR

- Contact local EMS, schedule and attend a class
- Contact local Fire Department, schedule and attend class
- Contact local school system, attend a class if provided
- Visit the Red Cross web site
- Research the internet for relevant instructional and tutorial media
- Practice techniques regularly in mock situations
- Review current standards frequently to discover modifications and implement them

Verify Insurance Policies

- Home insurance up to date
- Vehicle insurance up to date
- Life insurance in place
- Valuable assets protected
- Medical and Health insurance current
- Dental insurance current

- Inclement weather insurance in place
- Natural Disaster insurance plans in place

Collect & Copy Important Documents

- Driver's license
- State issued ID card
- SSN card
- Passport
- Credit/Debit card
- Bank routing and account numbers
- Bank statements (current)
- Insurance policies
- Financial assets (stocks, bonds, etc.)
- Birth Certificates

Establish Primary & Alternate Routes of Evacuation

- Maps (roads, highways, nature trails, and topographical terrain)
- Color code preferred routes
- Color code alternate routes (different color combinations)
- Travel the routes personally
- Look for obstacles that could complicate travel under dire circumstances

5.3 Prepare Your Inventory

Prepare Your Inventory

Make a List

- Describe the disaster
    - Natural
    - Manmade
    - Biological
    - Weather Related

Identify Items Already Procured

- Make a list of the supplies you currently have available for each of the categories above
- Identify areas of interest (missing, expired, or outdated equipment)
- Consider optional or substitute equipment for inclusion

Purchase Missing Products

- Identify the items that are missing from the essentials
- Find places where these items can be purchased
- Take the time to procure the items on the list

Rotate Food & Batteries

- Periodically check expiration dates on food items
- Periodically check charge of batteries

- Periodically check battery operated equipment
- Rotate, replenish, or replace any items that require it
- Check and refresh rechargeable batteries

Update & Modify List According to Changes

- Check with local, state, and federal establishments periodically
- Implement any recommended updates or changes offered
- Replace items that no longer apply to your plans
- Check with online disaster preparedness communities to keep up on world events and possibilities
- Be prepared to adapt, modify, and compensate for missing or broken gear
- Make amendments to the list if you relocate to a new city or state

5.4 Establish Family Contacts

Establish Family Contacts

Compile Contact Info for Family & Friends

- Immediate Family Members
  - o Parents
  - o Siblings/Children

- Extended Family Members
  - Grandparents
  - Aunts/Uncles
  - Cousins
  - Nephews/Nieces
- Friends & Associates
  - Co-workers
  - Neighbors
  - Business partners

Designate Rally Points

- Establish a Primary meeting place
  - Home
  - School
  - Place of Business
  - Storage Facility
- Establish secondary way points
  - Parks
  - Recognized Landmarks
  - Spots along the expected route of evacuation
  - Spots along all secondary or alternate routes
- Establish a final meeting place
  - Somewhere near the shelter
  - A suitable scouting location to ensure the integrity of the shelter
- Establish meeting times
  - How long after an event should the group wait at each point for stragglers
  - Establish communication for leaving messages for those following behind

Plan with Family & Friends

- Establish relationships with like-minded individuals
- Find out what steps they are taking
- Share advice and recommendations
- Discuss and agree on differences of opinion
- Make sure everyone involved is on the same page
- Provide detailed maps and instructions to everyone involved
- Schedule & Practice Mock-up scenarios with everyone included
- Identify areas of interest that need to be addressed and corrected
- Correct any problem areas identified in earlier practices
- Reschedule & Repeat practicing mock-up scenarios
- Review the preparedness plan frequently
- Adjust and modify responsive actions accordingly
- Practice until techniques become second nature
- Identify areas of responsibility and assign duties and tasks

Plan Practice & Maintenance

Educate All Family Members

- Make sure everyone is aware of what the preparedness plan involves
- Ensure all modifications/amendments are discussed and agreed upon
- Encourage positive discussions, creativity, and debate
- Incorporate ideas that appeal to your plan
- Ensure everyone knows their duties and accepts full responsibility

Pop-Quiz Family Members Every 6 Months

- Establish unscheduled testing of relevant information at least every 6 months
- Score the tests
- Identify areas of concern for everyone
- Make sure any adjustments/modifications are understood
- Re-educate those that need remedial training
- Re-test & evaluate

Run Mock-up Drills Frequently

- Schedule training events for various disasters in your area
- Make sure everyone can attend these functions
- Evaluate the outcome
- Perform unscheduled mock-up events
- Evaluate how family members respond to an unscheduled event
- Evaluate differences between scheduled and unscheduled events
- Make corrections as a group or individually as required

Rotate Stored Food & Water

- Rotate, replace, or replenish bug-out bag contents
- Rotate, replace, or replenish bug-out vehicle kit contents
- Rotate, replace, or replenish supplies stocked at the haven
- Use items before expiration to eliminate excessive waste

Update Plan According to Lifestyle Changes

- Relocation requires reacquiring relevant information for the region and adjusting the plan

- Addition or Subtraction from the family unit will require compensatory adjustments
- Financial events, good or bad, may require making modifications
- Getting married/divorced will require restructuring efforts
- Onset of a medical condition might involve slight or severe modifications
- Change of attitude or outlook of possible events

CHAPTER 6: Preparing for Family Members with Special Needs

6.1 Oxygen Supplies

Oxygen Supplies

Obtaining Oxygen Tanks

I. Local Medical Supply Companies
   a. Local business directory
   b. Telephone book
   c. News media advertising
   d. Online website or advertising
II. Online Distributors
   a. Drop ship suppliers
   b. Portable Oxygen Concentrators
III. Transporting & Handling Concerns
   a. Read manufacturer warning labels and instructions
   b. Adhere to prescribed and recommended methods of transport
   c. Inspect cylinder for damage, dents, gouges, leaks, or cracks
   d. Inspect valve and pressure relief mechanism
   e. Secure and seal protective caps on valves
   f. Use carts to secure containers in an upright position

    g. Ensure cylinders do not interfere with others

    h. Store away from heat or ignition sources

IV.   Disposal of Used Cylinders

    a. Oxygen tanks are combustible

    b. If possible return them to an approved facility

    c. In extremely dire circumstances discard them in areas where fire will not be present

Electrical back-up for Medical Equipment

Alternative Power Sources

I. Medical Grade UPS (Uninterrupted Power Supply) devices
   a. Local Medical Supply Company
   b. Online Medical Supply Distributors
II. Battery back-up devices
   a. Local Medical Supply Company
   b. Online Medical Supply Distributors
III. Emergency generators
   a. Portable
   b. Permanent
   c. Must have approved rating for powering equipment in question
   d. Requires an alternate fuel source
IV. Solar Power Systems
   a. May not always work depending on circumstances
   b. Permanent fixture (should be installed at a haven/survival bunker)

6.3 Copies of Prescriptions

Copies of Prescriptions

Medical History

I. Copies of all current prescriptions
   a. Photocopies of actual handwritten prescriptions from the attending physician
   b. Prescription bottles with labels indicating available refills
II. Copies of all previous history
   a. Duplicates of medical records
   b. Copies of past and present prescriptions
   c. Medicinal diary of any non-prescription medicines being taken in conjunction with prescriptions
III. Honesty of personal health
   a. Document all drug use (legal and illegal)
      i. Legal medication can interact adversely with street substances
   b. List physical ailments (minor & major)

6.4 Two weeks supply of prescription and non-prescription medicines

Two weeks supply of prescription and non-prescription medicines

Medications You Require

I. Two weeks supply of all current prescriptions
   a. Topical

        b. Oral
        c. Injections
        d. Medicated Eye Drops
            i. All of these should be brought along whether you use them or not

II. Two weeks supply of non-prescription medicines
        a. Aspirin
        b. Tylenol
        c. Cough Medication
        d. Flu Medication
        e. Eye drops (un-medicated)
        f. Any & All OTC supplements you are currently taking

Note: *Medication of any nature should not be abused or misused, nor should it be shared with others as it could have damaging or fatal results*

6.5 Two weeks supply of disposables

Two weeks supply of disposables

Items You Will Use and Discard Regularly

I. Bandages
        a. Gauze
        b. Band-aids (small cuts and gashes)
        c. Wound Dressings
        d. Surgical/Medical Tape
        e. Medical Super-Glue

II. Razors (Shaving hair from an affected area)

      a. Disposable
      b. Replaceable
      c. Quality over Quantity (Do not purchase the dollar variety three pack for this purpose)

III. Disinfectants/Sterilizers for cleaning wounds
      a. Glutaraldehyde
      b. Anti-bacterial wipes
      c. Mild Soap and Warm Water
      d. Betadine Solution (diluted with water accordingly)
      e. Hydrogen Peroxide (the bubbling action with help lift and clean small debris)

IV. Personal Protective Equipment
      a. Gloves
      b. Surgical Masks
      c. Clean Protective Garments (surgical attire; shoe covers, smock, or apron)
      d. Safety Glasses

6.6 For Hearing Impaired

For Hearing Impaired

Assistive Equipment for Communication Procedures

I. Lights
      a. Flashlights
      b. Penlights
      c. Disposable Lighters
      d. Candles

        i. Any source of visible light that will help them read since hearing is difficult.

II. Writing Instruments
- **a.** Pens
- **b.** Pencils
- **c.** Black Markers
  - **i.** Anything they can write with or that you can write with

III. Paper
- **a.** Notepads
- **b.** Ledgers
- **c.** Notebooks
- **d.** Diaries
- **e.** Small Portable Chalkboard
- **f.** Erasable White Board
  - **i.** Anything that can be written on

IV. Hearing Aids
- **a.** Spare hearing apparatuses
- **b.** Spare batteries

V. Establish a Buddy System
- **a.** Have a member of the family accept responsibility for communicating and interpreting with the hearing impaired so they are kept aware of what is taking place.
- **b.** Learn and educate all concerned members on how to properly use sign language

6.7 For Visually Impaired

For Visually Impaired

Assistive Equipment for Communication & Mobility

I.   Walking Implements
   a. Extra Cane
   b. Walker
   c. Buddy System (someone assigned to support the visually impaired individual)
   d. Leash (used as a guidance system to keep the visually impaired with the other members of the group when traveling by foot in single file formation or under less than perfect light environments)

II.   Communication
   a. Whistle (alerting them to a location)
   b. Buddy System (someone assigned to direct the impaired person or assist them with instructions)
   c. Glasses (prescription or readers if they will help them see more clearly)

III.   Buddy System
   a. Compensates for both categories above

CHAPTER 7: Bug Out or Bug In?

7.1 Shelter in Place

Shelter in Place

1. Locate suitable, sufficient, established, and approved places for gathering in your local community. (Regional Disaster Response)

2. Speak with family and friends in the community. Arrange for temporary shelter with them resulting from a house fire, storm damage, etc. (Localized Personal Property Loss Response)

3. Research different ideas regarding the construction of various survival shelters. Find a blueprint to follow. (Wide Spread Disaster Response)

4. Purchase additional land in a desired location away from pockets of civilization. Secure the property, (post No Trespassing signs, erect a fence as a boundary/barrier, and implement additional security, such as tripwires or pitfalls).

5. Buy the materials you will need to build your survival shelter. (Lumber, steel, concrete, various hand and power tools).

6. Schedule construction efforts. You will need to build your shelter, or have it built for you. (Always take matters

into your own hands if possible. The fewer people that know about your secret bug-out bunker, the safer and more secure it will be.)

7. Map out various routes of entry and exit. You may have to deviate from an established plan, under certain circumstances, to arrive at your temporary living quarters. It would be wise of you to have a couple of different methods available for ensuring everyone can eventually meet at the gathering place.

8. Stock & Storage of supplies. Your shelter should have enough supplies to sustain you and your family for longer than you would expect to stay. Non-perishable foods, potable drinking water, substitutions for household goods, such as spare blankets and bedding, kitchen utensils, fire producing resources and fuel, as well as additional clothing, should all be ready and waiting for your arrival.

__Note:__ The size of your shelter needs to comfortably accommodate you and your family. There are various disasters that could occur at any given time. Your plan of action should be determined by the circumstances at hand. You should plan on having several options for shelter at your disposal that will allow you to respond safely, sufficiently, and accordingly to all situations as soon as they arise.

7.2 Should I Stay, or Should I Go?

Should I Stay, or Should I Go?

1. Get familiar with the disaster plans of your community. Every county in the United States has a disaster preparedness plan in place for the citizens under their governance. These plans cover responsive steps and actions to take in the event a disaster strikes. The signaling alarms for each type of disaster, rally points, routes of travel, emergency contact numbers, media distribution resources, such as radio and television, will all be available in emergency response pamphlets or literature.

2. Make a checklist of all the areas of interest for each disaster that could occur. Have these checklists at your immediate disposal. Follow them to the letter whenever possible for the best chances of success. Deviation from the checklist should only be considered under extremely dire circumstances.

3. Remain calm, cool, and collected. This is easier said than done, especially with increasing levels of severity. Your composure when facing possible problems will determine how effective and efficient the outcome of your plan is. Panic and fear confuse and complicate matters, often leading to further, more complex issues to deal with.

4. Know when to go and when to stay. In some disaster scenarios it will be better for you to stay put rather than pack up and bug out. Severe weather patterns such as tornadoes, can occur rather rapidly; some affected residents will be able to flee the immediate vicinity as soon as an alarm or warning has sounded, others will be stuck or

stranded due to the confusion and congestion of unprepared participants.

5. Develop a family plan of action for handling all emergencies. Are the children old enough to understand and participate in activities of this nature? If so, then practice response drills for all situations, if not, then develop your plan(s) with the mindset of having to secure the kids along the route.

6. Make sure everything you need is in place. You cannot plan to bug out or stay put if you have nowhere to go and little or no supplies at your disposal. Know where your bug-out bags are and store them in a place or area they can be easily retrieved.

7. Your preparedness plans need to encompass possibilities for both leaving, and hunkering down for the long haul. The circumstances surrounding a disaster might call for evacuation; however, unforeseen problems may arise that prevent you from implementing your plan in its entirety. Have a back-up plan in place and be ready to change directions for your survival.

7.3 What Should I Include in My Evacuation Plan?

What Should I Include in My Evacuation Plan?

1. Your evacuation plan will be determined by what disaster is taking place. The items you need to have at your disposal for all these various scenarios will be similar in

several areas.

2. Evacuation means leaving, departing, getting out of the area as fast and safely as possible. The level of intensity or degree of disaster will dictate what you need to bring along.

3. House safety checklist. Are the windows and doors all locked or secured? Are all people and pets accounted for? Have essential services been shut off or disconnected, such as water, electricity, and heating resources?

4. Essentials. The clothes on your back as well as any personal belongings carried on your person.

5. Personal identification and financial information. Driver's license, state issued ID card, SSN card, passport and credit/debit cards. Color copies of all these items may also come in handy.

6. Your bug-out bag, which should have many of the items you will want or need along the route.

7. Maps of the travel routes. Be aware of the recommended routes of travel and regional rally points. Know what they are and use them when possible. Develop alternate routes, and have course plotted charts available in the event you need to deviate from the current course and still arrive at the desired location.

8. Communication devices. Not all disasters will be of the magnitude to destroy communication grids so bring along cell phones, portable radios, and mobile computing equipment that can function on cellular systems.

9. Plan for several modes of transportation. While the initial escape efforts might include piling everyone into a vehicle to make the get-away; traffic congestion or other unforeseen events may complicate completing the trip by automobile. Be prepared to abandon the vehicle and continue by foot. If you live near water, and the disaster isn't water related, consider evacuating by watercraft. Pack and draft animals might also be worthy of consideration for evacuation efforts. In extreme circumstances, everyone is going to be running for the hills using different types of transportation. A horse can be ridden, or used to pull a wagon, which could make your departure an uninterrupted event.

10. Emergency contact numbers for first responders, hospitals and trauma centers, should also be included in the plan. These numbers can be used to forewarn others of an inbound disaster, or to seek additional information if something from the approved battle plan has been altered, such as the relocation of the relief center.

7.4 Where Should I Go

Where Should I Go?

1. Where you end up will be determined solely by the disaster taking place in conjunction with how well prepared you and your family are at the time the event strikes.

2. Regional disaster response programs are available and in place for each county in the country.

3. Visit your local county disaster preparedness office/center. Request copies of all available literature involving approved and recommended response procedures for the citizens of the region.

4. Get familiar with major traffic routes as well as lesser traveled roadways and back alleys. The more information you have available, the better chance you have of arriving at point 'B' once you have left point 'A.' Everyone in the community will have access to the same information, they are all going to be attempting to utilize this information to the best of their abilities. This will undoubtedly result in confusion and congestion. Be prepared to circumvent these situations.

5. What do the circumstances call for? Do you need to evacuate en masse, along with everyone else in the surrounding area? Is the disaster of a personal nature affecting just you, your family, and your residence? Each situation will require a different response.

6. Are you confident and comfortable with the response plan the local governing body has established? If you are, then use it. It is always recommended to have a back-up plan. Massive shelter environments can become overcrowded. Overcrowding leads to increased interaction, which in turn can result in increased friction and/or factional problems, wherein different sects of survivors group together and work against the efforts of all others.

7. Is the disaster of a personal nature? Has the house been moderately damaged due to fire, flooding, or storm debris? You might seek shelter from a hotel/motel in the area; your insurance may even cover the cost of temporary

housing.

8. Do you have family or friends in the area? Consider making temporary arrangements to bunk down with them at their house for a few days.

9. Recreational vehicle. Do you have one available and suitable for your immediate needs? Relocate the family to the comfort and convenience of the backyard, or an RV park, for a few nights or longer.

10. A personally owned survival shelter. Have you built your storm shelter yet? Is it complete? Do you have ample supplies to accommodate the needs of you and your family? If so, then hit the highway! Make tracks and travel to your preferred destination.

11. Does anyone in the traveling party require extensive medical attention of the nature you are ill equipped to handle? Seek assistance at the emergency relief/trauma center or area hospital.

7.5 What Is A Safe House/Place?

What Is A Safe House/Place?

1. In laymen's terms, a safe house is a panic room on steroids. It provides protection from possible harm, as well as essential equipment and supplies, to ensure the survival of you and your family. It can be above ground or subterranean.

2. A safe house or place can have several different meanings depending on who you pose the question to. Ask a hundred different people, from a hundred separate locations, and you will likely receive several various answers.

3. A safe house is a place you can trust confidently and completely. You should never fear using your safe house, if it has been properly established.

4. Safe houses/places are pre-existing establishments or environments. It is an area or building that you have visited personally and ensured meets or exceeds your preferences and demands.

5. These facilities can be in all regions from rural to metropolitan.

6. A rural safe house allows you to stay further off the grid. Cover and concealment are advantageous for some situations. A rural region allows you to determine if/when you interact with society. Rural safe houses can be somewhat restrictive. If you interact with members of a small farming community, they are more likely to remember your face than are residents of a metropolis. You may have to limit your movements or make plans to secure any necessary supplies from a suburban setting nearby, if you intend to maintain a low profile.

7. A metropolitan safe house provides you with the opportunity to change identities and blend into the new surroundings. It will also allow you to continue using modern technology to your advantage should you need to monitor the activities of those trying to find you. It may also make it easier to slip away undetected. Thousands of

people clog the sidewalks of NYC and LA daily; should you need to make a hasty exit, you might be able to simply slip into the crowd and walk away.

8. Your safe house should be situated in a location that only you and your trusted associates are aware of. In other words, even if it is an existing structure that can be identified by people in the surrounding community, it should not be a place that your work associates are familiar with as your safe house. The fewer people that know your intentions for using this place, the better the safety and security of you and your family.

9. It should be an area not easily compromised. This is not a place you should frequent regularly. Set-up of a safe house should be conducted in a single event. You purchase or construct the habitat, stock it with necessary supplies, ensure everything is in order, then lock the door and walk-away. Avoid revisiting this area for any reason other than what it was intended for. The more you frequent the facility, the easier it will be to target and identify.

7.6 How Do I Get to My Safe House/Place?

How Do I Get to My Safe House/Place?

Off Road:

Regardless of where your safe house is situated, it may be necessary to plan for unconventional means of transportation. You cannot rely on established routes of travel for all disasters.

Walking / Hiking—be prepared to travel by foot. When current means of transportation fail, or become unserviceable, you will have to take to your heels. Comfortable foot attire will be instrumental in achieving success.

Pack / Draft Animals—consider riding horses or having draft animals to pull wagons for transportation in extreme circumstances. This is quicker than walking and will allow you to travel over rough and rugged terrain without exposing yourself to potential hazards along the way.

Bicycles—mountain bikes are built to be durable and can handle abusive use over rough and rugged terrain. This method is also faster than walking and allows you to transfer to foot if necessary without leaving a living creature behind, as would be the case above.

Recreational Vehicles—ATV's, dirt bikes, and/or snowmobiles (northern climates during winter season). These are smaller vehicles which can easily be used on or off road. They are fuel efficient, which allows you to travel trails to get from one spot to another, before needing to be refueled. They can also be abandoned in the event further travel by foot is required.

Watercraft—boats, canoes, kayaks, or in some cases a jet ski. Do you live near water? Is your safe house situated near a large body of water or river? Part of your travel plans might include using this type of equipment to cover your trail, or make a quick get-away, to an area where a better mode of transportation has been stored.

Bug-out Vehicle:

Automobile—any type of gas powered vehicle, some of which were mentioned above, can be used for a bug-out bus. Cars, trucks, or family vans that are equipped with the essential disaster preparedness kits will suffice for evacuation efforts.

Modified Mobility Equipment—believe it or not there are companies and individuals in the automotive industry that specialize in fabricating vehicles for the specific purpose of ensuring safety and security for those in the preparedness community. These can include reinforced conventional or recreational vehicles.

Aircraft—a small personally owned plane or helicopter can also be used for transportation from home to safe house under the right circumstances. You will need an airstrip for departure as well as landing, and the ability to fly below the radar to avoid filing a flight plan.

Note: Regardless of what mode of transportation you choose to use for reaching your safe house it should be in perfect working order. Equipment that needs repair should be avoided or compensated for with a back-up plan in the event it does fail. This vehicle needs to be able to carry you, and every member of your family, safely and securely. It should also be able to accommodate the bug out bag(s) that will provide for each member. All gas powered transportation equipment should also house additional fuel supplies in the event current stations are closed along a portion of the route. *(Aircraft may be exempt from storing additional fuel as proper planning should involve being able to get to the destination without making pit stops along the route; however,* *additional fuel should be stored at the safe house to allow for return, or additional departure, should the area be compromised).*

Survival Cache along the Route:

Your survival cache along the route should consist of supplemental supplies that are like the ones you are currently carrying. Non-perishable food, potable drinking water, tools, first aid supplies, additional fuel, and substitute transportation are all worthy of consideration. Even the best prepared planner can encounter obstacles they did not originally envision while developing a get-away plan to reach a safe house. What you thought might take 3-5 days could end up taking a week or longer.

7.7 What Do I Bring with Me?

What Do I Bring with Me?

Bug-out Bag(s)—these are your personal protection and survival systems. Contents of this equipment will vary; however, they should sustain the owner for a period of 3-5 days with essentials and necessities.

Bug-out Vehicle Kit—includes items necessary to ensure safe passage. Additional fuses, spark plugs, flashlights, flares, spare tire(s), automotive related tools for performing mechanical work, such as a jack, wrenches, pliers, and a utility knife, should all be included in this kit. A first aid kit is an optional consideration if not carried in the bag(s) mentioned above.

Tools—a small handbag with commonly used

equipment. Two screwdrivers, a Philips and a regular, a hammer, an adjustable wrench, pocket flashlight, and pocket knife, should be in this bag and situated in a place convenient for immediate access.

Food & Water Supplies—as mentioned previously non-perishable food sources and potable drinking water. A personal water filtration/purification system for everyone should also be considered.

Camping Gear—tents, sleeping bags, fire producing material, cooking utensils, fuel lamps for lighting, a small folding shovel, and a fire extinguisher make the short list of supplies in this category.

Extra Fuel & Oil—although covered previously, it warrants mentioning again. If you are traveling by gas powered equipment, then you need to ensure you have ample refueling resources to compensate for all events of an unforeseen or unexpected nature.

CHAPTER 8: Preparing with Family Pets

8.1 Planning Ahead

Planning Ahead

Making the Proper Preparations

- **Boarding Facilities**
  - Local area businesses that provide this service (temporary)
  - Extended family members with available time and space (temporary/permanent)
  - Neighbors with ample space and time (temporary/permanent)
  - Leaving them home (temporary, short periods of time if needs are provided for)
  - Quick, easy, convenient, and hassle free
  - Financially feasible with friends or family (professional services have various packages and prices)
  - Local animal shelters (some local county sponsored establishments provide temporary services)

- **Bring Them Along**
  - Build them a bug-out bag for their needs (food, water, medication)
  - Make sure there is ample space and equipment for transportation

- o Make sure it is realistic (ex. cats & dogs)
- o Eliminate unrealistic (ex. birds & fish)
- o How will they travel (cage/crate or free)?
- o Toys for entertainment
- o Increased responsibility
- o Extra mouths to feed

> **Setting Them Free**
>   - o Best chance at survival in some scenarios
>   - o Forage and fend for themselves
>   - o Reduction in occupied space
>   - o Eliminate the need to search for them (outdoor free roaming pets)
>   - o Reduced responsibility
>   - o Reduced supply list
>   - o Reduced weight
>   - o Less unwanted awareness
>   - ▪ People love pets, they are attracted to them
>   - ▪ People with distinctive pets are easier to identify
>   - ▪ Animals respond orally when triggered (complicates cover & concealment)

8.2 Red Cross Policy

Red Cross Policy

No Pets Allowed in Shelters

- ➢ **Pet Policy**
    - ○ Federal and state rules and regulations prohibit the American branch of the Red Cross from admitting domestic household pets
    - ○ Service animals are admitted (documentation of necessity may be requested)

- ➢ **Assistance Programs for Pets**
    - ○ Red Cross facilities have established guidance programs for helping you prepare to provide for your pets
    - ○ Employees will help you develop a plan of action for your pets (provide literature, offer advice, make recommendations)

8.3 Food & Water

Food & Water

Provisions

- ➢ **Planning for Provisions**

- o Supplying the family or friend boarding the pet with ample food supplies
- o Offering additional funds for extended stays
- o Bringing enough with you if they are coming along
  - Include snacks and treats in the equation
- o Animals can replenish water supplies from available natural resources if allowed to access them
- o Allow them to forage or fend for themselves (in the event they are being released)

➤ **Supplementing Provisions**
- o Pertains to bringing your pets along
- o Feeding them table scraps
- o Beef and/or pork bones (no chicken bones they splinter and kill animals)

8.4 Crate/Cage

Crate/Cage

Transporting/Containment

➤ **Temporary**
- o Portable
- o Easy to move/carry
- o Easy access door with locking mechanism
- o Feed trays (spill proof if possible)
- o Ample space for the pet (laying down, moving around)

- o Suitable for being carried with available equipment or methods of transportation
- o Sturdy
- o Durable
- o Ample venting without compromising containment
- o Comfortable for the pet (discomfort induces stress)
    - Should be used for transportation rather than containment at a permanent location

> **Permanent**
- o Larger containment facilities
- o House/kennel
- o Fenced in environment
- o Exercise equipment
- o Food & Water trays
- o Sturdy
- o Durable
- o Easy access for pet
- o Comfort equipment (bedding, blanket)
- o Better venting & visibility for the pet
- o Placed in a preferred/suitable location
    - A permanent shelter should be already in place at the destination
    - Should be used more for containment than transportation

8.5 Leash / Harness

Leash/Harness

Exercise/Control

- ➢ **Exercise**
  - o Walking
  - o Running
  - o Scouting/Hunting
  - o Hiking
    - ▪ Anything that involves bringing your pet along while on foot
  - o Safety & Security
    - ▪ For the pet
    - ▪ For passerby
    - ▪ For encountered wildlife
  - o Comfort
    - ▪ Does not harm the pet
    - ▪ Fits snugly without being too tight
    - ▪ Easy to fit and remove
    - ▪ Ample length of chain (allow freedom of movement)
    - ▪ Easy to control
    - ▪ Quick release attachment for collar

- ➢ **Control**
  - o Training purposes in a new environment
  - o Effectively commands the pet without inducing harm
  - o Easy to attach and release
  - o Sturdy
  - o Durable

- o   Harnesses over leashes

8.6 Pet Medications

Pet Medications

The Health of Your Pet is in Your Hands

- ➢ **Prescriptions**
  - o   Pills
  - o   Oral liquids
  - o   Eye medication
  - o   Vaccinations
  - o   Salves & Ointments
  - o   Medicated shampoos
    - ▪ An ample supply of these items need to be given to the boarding facility, family, or friend caring for the pet, or brought along with you
    - ▪ Provisions for refilling prescriptions if needed should be made in advance of departure if the pet is being boarded

- ➢ **Non-prescriptions**
  - o   OTC vitamin supplements
  - o   OTC flea & tick products
  - o   Shampoos & Powders
  - o   Grooming equipment
  - o   Vet First Aid kit

- o Splints
- o Bandages
  - These are items that are optional for inclusion when boarding or bringing your pet along

> **Schedule & Dosage**
  - o Adhere to the instructions of the prescription (Vet prescribed medicines)
  - o Ensure you have ample supply to compensate for your stay (two weeks supply should suffice, your pets are part of your family, treat them accordingly)
    - A schedule and dosage chart should be provided to any caregiver or brought along to keep track of records

8.7 Contact Info

Contact Info

Keeping in Touch with Your Pet

> **Names Numbers & Email Addresses for the Following**
  - o Veterinarian
  - o Boarding Facility
  - o Family/Friends
  - o Animal Shelter
    - This includes cellular and landline numbers

- If social network subscribers, account info for contact should also be included
  - o After hours emergency contact procedures
  - o Ensure the caregiver has all this information available for you as well
  - o Make a list of detailed instructions on actions to take in the event you cannot be consulted (pet needs an operation or humane euthanasia as the result of an accident or illness)

8.8 Pictures

Pictures of You & Your Pet

Search & Rescue

➢ **Identification Purposes**
  - o Finding lost pets after an event
  - o Identifies your pet and who is looking for them
  - o Copies can be distributed around shelters and communities
  - o Have your name and that of your pet
  - o Have all available contact information for you personally
  - o Have secondary contact information in the event you cannot be contacted
  - o Should include last known location

- o Include any identifying characteristics, markings, or habits not present in the photograph
- o Offer a reward for safe return **(optional)**

CHAPTER 9: Disaster Recovery Procedures

9.1 Returning Home

Returning Home

1) **Travel Plans**
    a. Maps (use the same ones that got you to the safe house/place. Make sure they have been modified to include obstacles encountered along evacuation journey)
    b. Food supplies (the return trip home could take just as long as the journey to get away. Ensure you have secured the same amount of supplies that got you there)
    c. Water (use your water purification devices as described above as bottled water supplies may be unavailable)
    d. Be prepared for unknown encounters along the way (depending on circumstances while you were away, the landscape may have changed drastically, making it difficult to identify previous landmarks)
    e. Have a compass handy for navigating through unfamiliar terrain
    f. Be prepared to augment modes of transportation (the vehicles and methods you used, and left along the route, may or may not be where you left them)

g. Weather the storm (do not return home before the affected area has been approved)

2) Collection & Cleanup of Safe House

a. Collect supplies (retrieval of items you will need to make the journey home)

b. Arrange Inventory (place all storable supplies in their proper place. Make a list of supplies consumed during your stay; they will need to be replenished as soon as possible to keep the shelter serviceable)

c. Cleanup the area you occupied (do not just abandon camp and leave all your clutter for another day. The urge to return home after an area has been declared "all clear," will be overwhelming, avoid acting on impulse; leftover food and debris will attract wildlife, or at the very least, alert others passing the premises of recent occupancy)

d. Ensure the safe house is secure (lock down all equipment and protective security devices. Use a checklist to complete the process)

e. Depart the facility (leaving just as it was when you arrived)

3) Expectations upon Arrival

a. Be prepared (damage/total loss of all property and structures may be evident; looting is also a common occurrence during disaster situations. Even if everything appears normal on the outside, items may have been removed)

b. Community Rebuilding & Support (regional residents returning to communities involved in a catastrophe tend to unite and organize relief efforts; find out where these temporary organizations are located, volunteer services, and/or request them)

c. Federal Assistance Programs (when an area has been devastated the federal government often enacts policies and procedures for implementing assistance programs for the residents affected. Find out if they are available and how to request them)

d. Resuming Normalcy (you will want to make sure that all essential services are restored and in good working order. Damaged equipment will need to be repaired, removed, or replaced. Any faults found in supply company components will need to be reported immediately)

e. Physical Checklist (have checklists available detailing contents for each room that were left behind when the evacuation occurred. This will assist in accounting for all items and discovery of what is missing)

f. Contacts (make sure to let all extended family members, friends, and associates know that you have returned safely to your normal domicile. Provide them with reassurance and closure)

9.2 Crisis Counseling

Crisis Counseling

1) **Is it Necessary?**
    a. Depends on circumstances (not all disasters require crisis counseling for the affected members of a region or area. It is available should the need be required)
    b. Group Therapy (often offered in disaster stricken areas after an event to educate the affected residents in various areas of interest)
    c. Individual Therapy (counseling obtained at personal expense to assist an individual with personal problems stemming from the event.)
    d. Family Counseling (obtained at personal expense to assist the entire family with understanding the events that took place. Also to assist with grieving in the event casualties were experienced)

***Note:** Crisis Counseling revolves around an individual or groups reaction to an adverse event of a disastrous nature, not to the actual disaster itself. It is intended to assist the affected member(s) with coping with the after effects of the situation. If an individual is mentally and emotionally capable of compensating for events without suffering consequences, they do not necessarily require counseling of this nature.*

2) **What does it provide the family?**
    a. Assistance (it will help adults understand why they are responding to the events in the way that they are. It will assist them with

developing plans of action to compensate for these responses. Also assists parents with educating and explaining things to their children)

b. A safe and secure environment (a place they can express their feelings and deepest fears without the worry of being ridiculed)

c. Trust (counselors help restore trust. Events that may have occurred during the evacuation may have caused a rift between two or more members of the family. To restore that bond, it is often necessary to seek an outside mediator)

d. Reassurance (Families that experience disasters often feel as though they were targeted personally, "Why did this happen to us?" They need to be reassured they were not responsible for the event)

e. Closure (it can help the family bring closure to the situation as well as assist them in returning to a level of normalcy in their everyday lives)

9.3 Dealing with Child Fears After a Disaster

Dealing with Child Fears after a Disaster

✓ *Separation from Family*—young children are often extremely confused, worried, scared, and under more stress than they let on. They have developed a bond with their parents and siblings. Disasters are a violent, devastating, and unfamiliar environment for everyone involved, especially the younger generations. They depend on their parents and older siblings for many of their needs. Even if they do not experience personal tragedies, such as the loss of a loved one during the event, they often hear stories of others that did, some of them told by people their age at school and on the playground. This can be a difficult and troubling topic to discuss. Family crisis counseling, and support services may be the best solution for helping educate children and calm their fears in this regard.

✓ ***Reoccurrence of Disaster***—this is a major fear among younger children. If it happens once it can happen again. Crisis counseling services may be advantageous in this area as well. Depending on the age of the child and their cognitive abilities, home education may also suffice. Statistical charts related to historical data related to the disaster, and frequency of events regarding region, can help conquer fear in this category. Relocating to another city, state, or region might also assist with calming issues of concern related to disaster reoccurrence; however, it is not always the solution, nor is it always financially feasible to uproot the family and move. Children need to be reassured that if they survived the incident once they can do so again. Build confidence to replace the fear.

✓ ***Injury or Death of a Loved One***—this is an all too real possibility when disaster strikes regardless of how well prepared and planned out the emergency response and evacuation happens to be. People die naturally every day, with or without an event occurring. This statistic is often magnified on a grand scale when a wide spread region is directly impacted by an emergency. The more volatile and violent the events, the greater chance of death there is. Parental counseling and comfort of the children is necessary. Family counseling may also be in order, as well as individual counseling for each affected member. This is a topic all of us hope we never have to deal with. Unfortunately it cannot be swept under the rug and avoided if the mental and emotional health of the family is to be restored.

✓ *Abandonment*—children also fear being abandoned after a disaster strikes. They may have experienced episodes during the events in which they were instructed to stay put while parent(s) forged ahead to scout or search and secure additional supplies and equipment. They may fear that this will happen again. If they experienced the death of one or both parents during the disaster, they may fear being placed up for adoption or sent to a shelter. They need to be reassured that all efforts are being made to place them with caring and loving extended family members. They will also need to be reassured that their new caretakers aren't going to experience the same demise and leave them in another awkward situation. Individual counseling, as well as group therapy, may be in order and effective for handling these fears and concerns.

CHAPTER 10: Best Recommendations

10.1 Sanitation

Sanitation

- ◆ **Areas of Interest**
  - ☼ Privacy
  - ☼ Accompaniment of Toiletries
  - ☼ Odor Control
  - ☼ Location of Facility
  - ☼ Comfort of Facilities
  - ☼ Control of Pollution
    - ▪ Dissolves into Ground Water Supplies
    - ▪ Poses Health Issues to Humans

- ◆ **Where to Conduct Daily Duties**
  - ☼ During the Journey
    - ▪ Available Restroom Facilities at Relief Centers
    - ▪ Along the Trail
    - ▪ Downstream
    - ▪ Downwind
  - ☼ Temporary Survival Shelter
    - ▪ Downstream
    - ▪ Dig a Ditch Downwind
    - ▪ Use Outhouse Facilities
      - • Hand Built

- Prefabricated Plastic Injection Models (seen at fairs, outdoor concerts etc.)
- ☼ Permanent Survival Shelter
  - Septic Field
  - Dry Composting Plumbing Fixtures
  - Military Style Field Latrines & Techniques (always located downwind)

10.2 Cooking

Cooking

- ♦ **Indoor**
  - ☼ Cast Iron Wood Burning Stoves
  - ☼ Propane Stoves

- ♦ **Outdoor**
  - ☼ Grills (Propane or Charcoal)
  - ☼ Portable Propane Stove
  - ☼ Fire Pits with Tripod Cooking Systems
  - ☼ Open fire pits
  - ☼ Hobo Stoves
  - ☼ Rocket Stoves

10.3 Illumination

Illumination

- **Indoor**
  - ☼ Candles
  - ☼ Flashlights
    - ■ Battery Operated
    - ■ Hand Crank
  - ☼ Fire (if fireplace is available)

- **Outdoor**
  - ☼ Fire (in approved fire pit)
  - ☼ Oil Lamps
  - ☼ Flashlights
    - ■ Battery Operated
    - ■ Hand Crank
  - ☼ Glow Sticks
  - ☼ Solar Powered Lighting

10.4 Shelter

Shelter

- **Indoor**
  - ☼ Tow Behind Camper
  - ☼ Truck Bed Camper
  - ☼ Truck Bed with Topper
  - ☼ RV
  - ☼ Established Safe House/Relief Center

- ♦ **Outdoor**
    - ☼ Tent
    - ☼ Half-shelters (tarps)
    - ☼ Zero Weather Sleeping Bag
    - ☼ Enclosed Hammock
    - ☼ Primitive Shelter Constructions

10.5 Heating

Heating

- ♦ **Cooking**
    - ☼ Fire
    - ☼ Propane

- ♦ **Personal Warmth**
    - ☼ Warm Clothing
    - ☼ Blankets
    - ☼ Glove Warmers
    - ☼ Body Heat (huddling together)
    - ☼ Single Candle

10.6 Clothing

Clothing

- ◆ **Durability**
  - ☼ Long Lasting
  - ☼ Tear Resistant
  - ☼ Quick Drying
  - ☼ Light Weight
  - ☼ Environmentally Effective
  - ☼ Climate Controlled

- ◆ **Foot Wear**
  - ☼ Comfortable
  - ☼ Durable
  - ☼ Serviceable for the Situation
    - ▪ Hiking Boots
    - ▪ River Shoes
  - ☼ Lightweight
  - ☼ Quick Drying
  - ☼ Supportive

- ◆ **Rotating**
  - ☼ Replace Stored Clothing
    - ▪ Seasonal Weather Changes
    - ▪ Lack of Use
      - ● Children outgrow clothes
      - ● New items come onto the market
  - ☼ Washing Stored Clothing
    - ▪ Removal of Dust & Mites
    - ▪ Place in a Convenient Location

- Reintroduction to Inventory when Seasons Change Again

Conclusion

The information offered in this guide is intended to provide you with the basic steps to implementing a disaster preparedness or survival plan. It should in no way to be misinterpreted as a complete and conclusive vessel encompassing every aspect, idea, list, or piece of equipment to be included for all events or situations.

This guide should deliver enough relevant and pertinent information to point you in the right direction for discovering additional education and data. It is the sole responsibility of the individual reader to apply or neglect any and/or all parts of this publication as they see fit. There are various degrees of disaster, as well as various outcomes and scenarios. The author of this guide and checklists, assumes no responsibility or liability for any issues or instances resulting from actions implemented, which were derived from the consumption of information in these pages.

You are free to use this guide to the best of your abilities. You will notice that portions of this guide are modified with bullet statements or numbered lists. This is to make it easier for the reader to identify areas of interest quickly and effectively, for helpful hints and recommended suggestions, without having to reread entire chapters or paragraphs. Similarly you will find some of the information listed repetitively in different categories. This was performed for the reader's benefit as well for accessibility and ease of use, as much of the information is relevant in either a general or specific nature.

You Are Now Aware

Disasters Can Happen Any Time and Any Where

Best of Luck in Your Preparations and Efforts

Always Remember

Failure to Plan = Planning to Fail

List of Resources

American Red Cross
www.redcross.org

Federal Emergency Management Agency (FEMA)
www.fema.gov

National Oceanic and Atmospheric Administration (NOAA)
www.noaa.gov

National Weather Service (NWS)
www.nws.noaa.gov

U.S. Department of Homeland Security
www.ready.gov
www.whitehouse.gov/homeland

Centers for Disease Control and Prevention (CDC)
www.cdc.gov

Citizen Corps
www.citizencorps.gov

USDA Food Safety and Consumer Information
www.fsis.usda.gov/OA/consedu.htm

http://vm.cfsan.fda.gov/~mow/intro.html

Food Safety.gov (part of the National Food Safety Information Network)

www.foodsafety.gov/~fsg/fsgadvic.html

American Academy of Pediatrics

www.aap.org

National Flood Insurance Program

1-800-427-4661

DISCLAIMER AND/OR LEGAL NOTICES: Every effort has been made to accurately represent this book and it's potential. Results vary with every individual, and your results may or may not be different from those depicted. No promises, guarantees or warranties, whether stated or implied, have been made that you will produce any specific result from this book. Your efforts are individual and unique, and may vary from those shown. Your success depends on your efforts, background and motivation. The material in this publication is provided for educational and informational purposes only. Use of the programs, advice, and information contained in this book is at the sole discretion and risk of the reader

9 781723 352690